A Clown in Town

by Dina McClellan
illustrated by Len Epstein

Core Decodable 96

McGraw Hill Education

Bothell, WA • Chicago, IL • Columbus, OH • New York, NY

MHEonline.com

Send all inquiries to:
McGraw-Hill Education
8787 Orion Place
Columbus, OH 43240

ISBN: 978-0-02-145188-3
MHID: 0-02-145188-5

Printed in Canada.

9 10 11 12 KOD 24

Rain showers are good for flowers, but not for the Brown family. The Browns were tired of being inside.

"How can we see clowns?" asked Howie.

"Is the circus in town?" asked Dad.

"Yes! There are clowns at the circus in town," said Mom.

The Browns ran down the stairs and rode the bus to town.

It was hot and crowded, but the Browns did not care.

Chowder the Clown did tricks. He made a cat bark and a dog meow.

The Browns took the bus out of town. On the way home, Howie said, "Wow! Clowns are much better than rain showers."